ANIMALS THAT HELP US

Animals as Carers

Clare Oliver

W

FRANKLIN WATTS
NEW YORK • LONDON • SYDNEY

First published in 1999 by
Franklin Watts
96 Leonard Street
London
EC2A 4XD

Franklin Watts Australia
14 Mars Road
Lane Cove
NSW 2066

Copyright © Franklin Watts 1999

ISBN 0 7496 3318 2

Dewey Decimal
Classification Number: 636

A CIP catalogue record for this book is
available from the British Library

Series editor: Helen Lanz
Series designer: Louise Snowdon
Picture research: Sue Mennell
Special Needs consultant: Dr. Philip Sawney

Printed in Malaysia

Contents

Extra care

Have you ever wondered why there is often a fish tank in the dentist's waiting room? Watching fish swim around helps people to relax and stops them thinking about having their teeth drilled.

Other pets can help us to feel better, too. Having to look after an animal — whether it is a small tortoise or large pony — is a big responsibility. It helps to make us feel wanted. We take care of ourselves, so we are fit to look after our pets.

Some people need extra care because they have special needs — and animals can help them as well.

People who can't see, for example, may use dogs to guide them. Dogs have also been trained to help people who find it hard to hear.

For people who are physically disabled (who have difficulty moving) working with animals improves their co-ordination and builds their confidence.

Riding is good exercise and improves balance.

Eyes that see

The very first guide dogs for blind people were trained in Germany after the First World War (1914-1918). Soldiers who had been blinded during the war were given guide dogs to help them in their daily lives.

An American woman called Mrs Harrison Eustis realized that all blind people – not just soldiers – would find a dog a useful companion.

Mrs Eustis set up *'L'Oeil Qui Voit'* ('the eye that sees') in Switzerland – the very first organization that trained guide dogs for blind people.

Mrs Eustis travelled all over the world to talk about her work.

Animal Anecdote

Morris Frank became the first guide dog owner in the United States. With the help of Mrs Eustis, he learnt how to work with Buddy, his guide dog.

Buddy was trained in Switzerland and was then taken to the United States to be with Morris Frank.

Dogs are excellent at this sort of work. They enjoy being with people, they learn quickly and they are usually obedient, keen to do as they are told.

Today, there are schemes for training guide dogs worldwide. This man and his guide dog live in South Korea.

Puppy programme

Puppies start the guide dog training when they are 6 weeks old.

Not all the puppies put forward for the training programme will be chosen. Each puppy is tested to see whether it is gentle, and whether it is clever enough for the job.

Labradors and Golden Retrievers are the most popular guide dog breeds.

The puppy lives with a 'puppy walking' family for the first year. Family members make sure the puppy learns to recognize as many sights and sounds as possible. They take it to busy shopping centres, train stations, restaurants — and obedience classes.

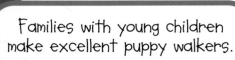

Families with young children make excellent puppy walkers.

If the puppy shows it can learn quickly, it goes back to the training centre. Here, it is shown how to travel on buses and trains. It is taught to walk around things that a person would not be able to walk under, such as railings. By the end of its training, the dog will understand about 20 commands.

The dog is taught to disobey a command that would lead its handler into danger.

The dog spends the final four weeks of its training with its owner-to-be, getting used to his or her voice. The owner is also trained in how to handle the dog. It is usually the beginning of a long, rewarding friendship.

Each dog learns to obey spoken commands and tugs of its harness.

9

Horse sense

Horse riding might seem a difficult hobby for someone who cannot see, but it is an excellent way for blind people, as well as sighted people, to relax and build up their confidence.

Grooming, as well as riding the horses, helps people learn how to handle the animals.

Horses that are ridden by blind people are chosen for their quiet, gentle natures. Horses that are easily scared are no good for this kind of work.

Often, the horses have already had one career working with people. Many horses in riding schools for blind people are police horses who are too old for police work. These horses have already had a lot of training and are always well-behaved.

Police horses are used to heavy traffic and won't jump or rear up at sudden noises.

The horses have more training at the riding school. They must learn to be very careful with their riders. Blind riders cannot see a low-hanging branch that could knock them out of the saddle. The horses are trained to walk around any dangers like this.

Instructors encourage the riders to do as much as they can for themselves.

Hearing dogs

For people who have difficulty hearing, a trained dog companion can make a big difference. 'Hearing dogs' have been used for over 20 years. Today there are training programmes for hearing dogs all over the world.

Like a guide dog, a hearing dog has a close friendship with its owner.

The dog's first task each day is to nudge its owner awake when it hears the alarm clock go off. All through the day the dog alerts its owner whenever there is a noise that the owner needs to respond to.

The dog touches its owner with its paw if the oven timer goes off, or the baby cries. It leads its owner to someone who is calling from another room, or to the door if the bell rings.

Both dog and owner are trained together.

Animal Anecdote

Usually, hearing dogs lead their owners to a sound — but not when it's a smoke alarm. Shirley-Ann's hearing dog, Max, knew just what to do when he heard the smoke alarm go off next door. He touched Shirley-Ann on her leg and then lay down — the sign for danger. Thanks to Max, the fire brigade was called and the fire was put out.

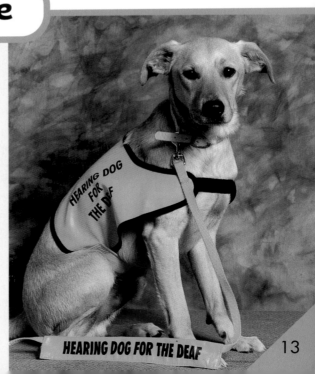

Max was given an award for his quick thinking.

HEARING DOG FOR THE DEAF

13

Training hearing dogs

Most hearing dogs are mongrels. The breed of dog does not matter, as long as the animal is bright and good-tempered.

Like guide dogs, hearing dogs start their training by living with a family.

Families who take hearing dogs are called 'socialising families'. This dog was the 1000th puppy to be placed with a family in the UK.

Many of the dogs are from rescue centres. They have often been left by their first owner. With time and patience they can become good hearing dogs.

Serious training starts once the dog has been taught basic obedience skills.

Each dog is taught different commands, depending on the special needs of its new owner.

The dogs learn by being praised when they do the right thing.

The dog learns the sound of its own door bell and leads the trainer to the door when it rings. Each dog is also taught not to do anything if it hears a different type of door bell.

After training the dogs are given a yellow coat to wear to show that they are fully-trained hearing dogs for a deaf person.

When out and about, hearing dogs wear their yellow jackets.

Assistance pets

People who are physically disabled find some everyday tasks very frustrating. Living with an assistance pet can make a real difference. The animal is trained to help with certain tasks – and is a friend to its owner as well.

Monkey helpers have proved so useful that their owners are able to work from their own homes.

Capuchin monkeys make good assistance pets. Because monkeys have hands like ours they are able to do things that would be impossible for any other animal. They are clever enough to use machines – such as CD, tape and video players.

Dogs make very good assistance animals, too. Golden Retrievers and Labradors are chosen for their friendly, calm natures. They like to fetch and carry things – important tasks for all assistance animals.

The dogs are trained to pick things up, get things out of bags and carry the shopping.

Assistance dogs are more than everyday helpers. They make their owners feel safe, and they give them a new sense of freedom. And, above all, they are good companions.

On the job

Monkeys that are chosen to be assistance pets spend the first five years living as part of a volunteer family. Then the tame monkeys spend a year at a training centre. There they learn to recognize commands to do many different tasks.

Most monkey helpers are bred at centres where they are specially-trained for the job.

Dogs also go through different stages of training. Suitable puppies are chosen and placed with a volunteer puppy walking family for a year. The dogs then continue their training for a further six months at a training centre. Here they learn over 90 spoken commands.

Dogs can help when things are difficult to reach.

It's important that each trained animal is matched carefully with its new owner. The owner and assistance dog go on a two-week training course. Someone will then visit them in their home to make sure the partnership is working.

The owner and dog stay together only if they get on well with each other.

Animal Anecdote

After Allen's car accident he was introduced to Endal, an assistance dog. Endal helps Allen to dress by fetching his clothes for him. He also helps Allen around the house.

'Having Endal helped me to accept that I had a disability,' says Allen. 'But best of all, being responsible for Endal has stopped me thinking about myself all the time.'

The power to move

Riding a horse can help people with physical disabilities, and can also be great fun. Riders can enjoy the thrill of being on horseback. At the same time, they can concentrate on exercising certain muscles or parts of the body.

Someone always walks by the side of the horse. This helps the riders to feel safe. They know that someone is there to catch them if they fall.

The riding teachers choose exercises that suit each person's needs. Someone who does not have good balance might learn to move from facing forward to facing backwards on the horse as it walks on slowly. Or the person might be asked to lean forward and pat the horse.

In time, riders build up the confidence to go over jumps and enter competitions.

Animal Anecdote

Dan has cerebral palsy, a condition where his brain has difficulty controlling the movement of his body's muscles.

Dan says, 'I love it when I am on a horse. When I sit in the saddle and the horse starts to move, I feel free!'

Making friends

Some people have learning difficulties. They might not be able to concentrate on one thing for very long, or be able to follow instructions.

Riding in groups is fun.
You meet lots of new people.

People with learning difficulties sometimes find it hard to be with other people. They may not like to talk, or find it upsetting if there is any change in their routine.

Horse-riding can be a good way to encourage people with these special needs to mix with others. Riders discover that a simple 'kissing' noise can urge the horse to move again after it has stopped. They learn that by making a sound, they have the power to make things happen.

Children often become friends with their horses and soon learn to form friendships with other people, too.

Animal Anecdote

Heather was only three years old when she started riding. To begin with, she didn't want to get on to Allison the horse, but once she was in the saddle, she was soon enjoying herself.

Before she started riding, Heather hardly talked at all. She learnt that she could control what Allison did by saying commands. After two years of riding, Heather is a chatterbox – but her very favourite words are 'Allison' and 'horse'.

23

Swimming with dolphins

At the Human Dolphin Therapy Centre in Miami, in the United States, children with learning difficulties swim with dolphins – and the dolphins seem to work magic.

Children usually spend two weeks at the centre. Therapists work with the children to improve their speech and massage their bodies. And the children swim with the dolphins every day. Just being with the dolphins relaxes the children.

Some experts think that it makes the children feel special that such beautiful, wild creatures want to spend time swimming with them. Perhaps it's not surprising that sharing the dolphins' games has a magical effect on people.

Dolphins enjoy playing with other dolphins, too. They are wonderful to watch in the wild.

Animal Anecdote

Nikki was born in 1990 with brain damage. Until 1998 he had never spoken a single word. Then he went swimming with dolphins in the Miami Centre in the United States. Amazingly, after just a few swims, Nikki spoke his first word. He said 'in' – because he wanted to get back in the water to be with the dolphins.

Special powers

People with epilepsy live full lives like everyone else. Epilepsy is a condition where the brain produces too many messages at once. When this happens the person can become unconscious and fall — this is called a seizure.

Someone with epilepsy may have a seizure without any warning. It can be very dangerous if the person falls in an awkward place.

Often we do things that could be very dangerous if we had a seizure.

A seizure alert dog can sense that a person is going to have a seizure about half an hour before it happens. The dog is trained to warn its owner that a seizure is coming on.

When the dog senses a seizure is going to happen, it may stare, bark or paw at its owner as a warning.

The person then knows to find a place where he or she will not be hurt if a seizure starts.

Having a seizure alert dog allows people with epilepsy to do things they otherwise would not have the confidence to do.

Owners and dogs have a strong friendship.

Pets as therapy

People who live on their own often feel lonely. This can happen to anyone at any age — whether they are old or young. Feeling that no one cares is hard — and then a pet's endless love can make a big difference.

A pet provides good company in return for being well looked after.

PAT (Pets As Therapy) animals are ordinary pets who live with ordinary families. But once or twice a week they go and visit people in nursing homes or hospitals. Dogs, cats and even rabbits are used — the main thing is that the animal is gentle and friendly towards strangers, and enjoys being petted.

This bunny visitor has certainly brought a smile to its friend's face!

Some children's homes have mini-farms where there are many different animals such as chickens, ducks and sheep. The children enjoy holding and stroking the animals, and they also learn to look after them.

It's the children's responsibility to keep the animals clean, fed and happy. Often, for the first time in their lives, the children have someone who depends on them.

Glossary

achievement   when you have completed a task you set yourself.

breed   a type of animal within an animal family; a Labrador is a breed of dog.

commands   words that tell someone else what to do.

confidence   a sense of believing in yourself.

disobey   not to do as you are told.

good-tempered   to have a nice nature, never being cross or grumpy.

grooming   the action of brushing or combing something, making it look smart.

handler   a person who looks after, trains and 'handles' an animal.

harness   straps around an animal's body that are attached to a lead to make the animal easy to control.

nature   the way someone or something behaves.

obedient   when you do as you are told.

unconscious   when someone is not awake or is unaware of what is happening.

Useful addresses

UK

Canine Partners for Independence
Homewell House
22 Homewell
Havant Hants PO9 1EE

Tel: 01705 450156

The Guide Dogs for the Blind Association
Hillfields, Burghfield Common
Reading Berkshire RG7 3YG

Tel: 0118 983 5555

Hearing Dogs for Deaf People
The Training Centre
London Road
Lewknor Oxon OX9 5RY

Tel: 01844 353898

Riding for the Disabled
Lavinia Norfolk House
Avenue R
National Agricultural Centre
Stoneleigh Park
Warwickshire CV8 2LY

Tel: 01203 696510

Support Dogs
The John Fisher Centre
Trianco House
Thorncliffe Park Estate
Chapeltown
Sheffield S35 2PH
Tel: 0114 257 7997

Australian addresses

Guide Dog Association
5 Northcliff Street
Nelsons Point
Sydney
NSW 2061

Tel: 02 99224211

RSPCA Sydney
201 Brookwood Road
Yagoona
PO Box 34
Yagoona
NSW 2199

Tel: 02 97095433

Index